I CHOOSE
to Speak Up

I CHOOSE SERIES

ELIZABETH ESTRADA

I CHOOSE
to Speak Up

ELIZABETH ESTRADA

I am not the same as you.
You're not the same as **me**.
For everyone is different.
And sometimes, we won't **agree**.

We come in many shades of skin,
Black, brown, tan, or **white**.
My face is not like yours.
And that's perfectly **alright**.

We may speak different languages
And come from foreign **lands**.
Or we might talk in different accents
That are hard to **understand**.

The foods we like can vary,
From the savory to **sweet**,
With dishes that you might enjoy,
But I might never **eat**.

There's rich and poor among us,
And also young and **old**.
Some might prefer the weather hot,
Or really like the **cold**.

We come in different shapes and sizes,
Like round or super **lean**,
Or short or tall or none of them,
But somewhere in **between**.

Some of us have hearing aids
Or have poor **eyesight**.
It doesn't matter, we're all the same.
There's no wrong or **right**.

You might have trouble focusing,
Or you're really, really **smart**.
You could be good at science,
Math, or excellent at **art**.

And some are quite athletic,
Always running here and **there**.
While others may have a handicap,
And they get to use a **wheelchair**.

The world is full of differences.
We see them **everyday**.
We're not all alike, and that's a good thing.
You're special in your own **way**.

But though we might be different,
There is no excuse for **hate**.
Discrimination is a thing
I'll never **tolerate**.

I just cannot stay in silence
When I know I have a **choice**.
I will tackle an injustice
With a clear and kind **voice**.

I can ask the person to stop
Who is hateful from **within**,
And doesn't see others
But for the color of their **skin**.

Or letting an adult know of
A bully who is full of **threats**,
And thinks they have the right
To take whatever they can **get**.

I can walk away from the person
Who is being hurtful and **unkind**,
Who thinks that they're
Superior in body or in **mind**.

I will speak up for a stranger.
I will speak up for a **friend**.
For myself, and all my family,
On that, you can **depend**.

And I'll battle for my principles
And all that I **believe**,
With a bit of courage,
Who knows what I'll **achieve**.

As the world is made for everyone,
And shouldn't be **unfair**.
I speak up against injustice
Because I truly **care**.

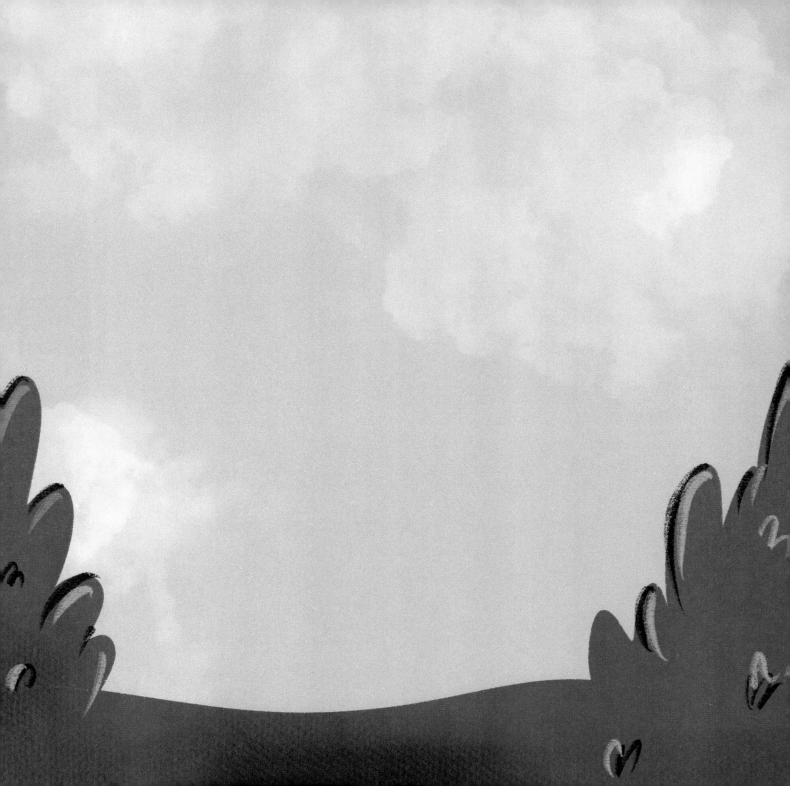

Made in the USA
Las Vegas, NV
28 September 2023

78241886R10024